DAD JOKES? I THINK YOU MEAN RAD JOKES!

101 NEW JOKES, FOR THE NEW YEAR!

ELIAS HILL

ILLUSTRATIONS BY: KATHERINE HOGAN

What type of fruit has to get married with family and friends present?

A cantaloupe.

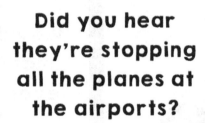

Did you hear they're stopping all the planes at the airports?

Yeah, so people can get on and off.

Earlier today a man broke into a house and released all the dogs.

Police are desperately looking for leads.

If I hear you slam the doors one more time...

I'll be really upset 'cause that's my favorite band.

Lancelot and King Arthur arrive at a motel.

Lancelot says, "We'd like a room for two knights, please."

Why did the chicken cross the road, roll in the mud, and cross the road again?
Because he was a dirty double-crosser.

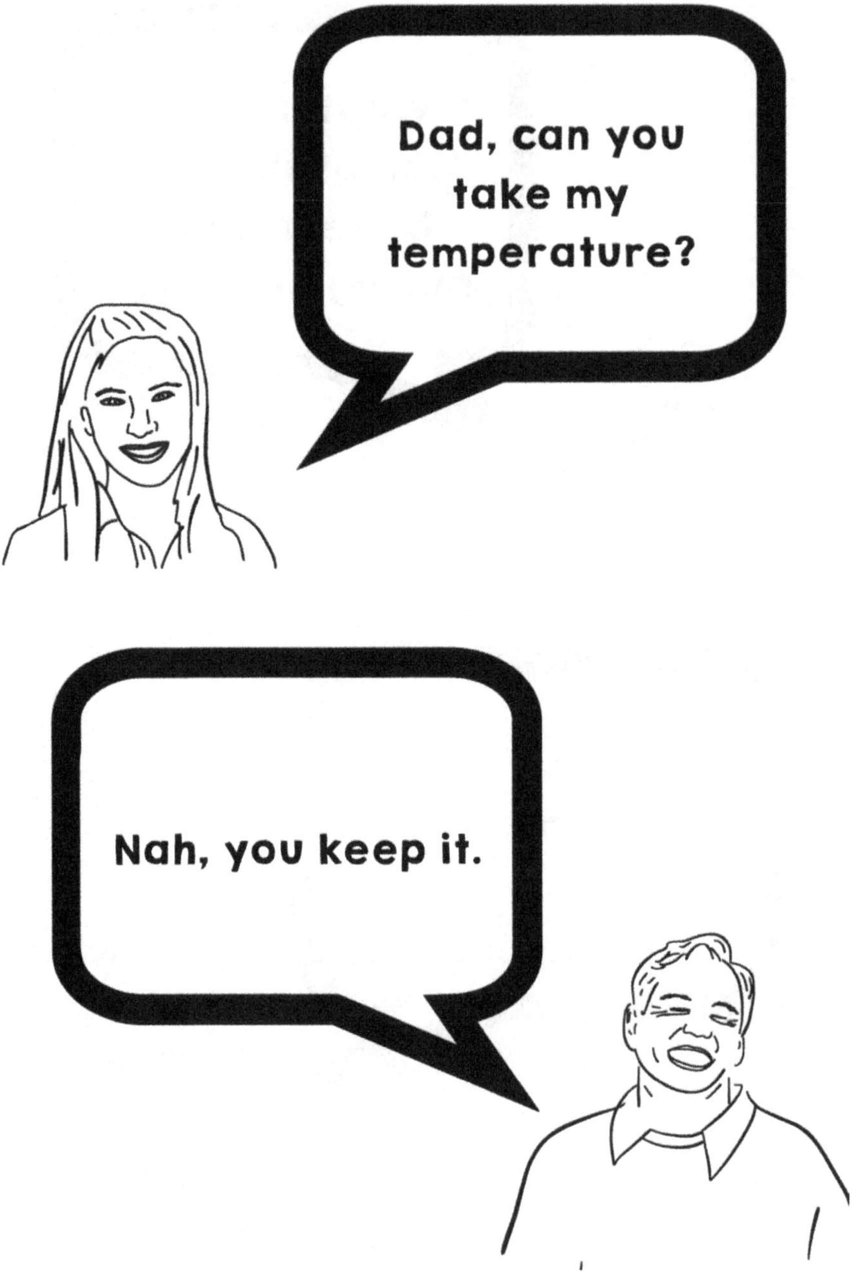
Dad, can you take my temperature?
Nah, you keep it.

How do you get
a sea creature
to play music?

You tuna fish.

What do you call the illegal trafficking of carbon dioxide?

Smoggling.

What do you call a vegetable that helps direct a film?

A producer.

Why did the devil rip apart the shoe?

He only wanted the sole.

My son keeps chewing on electrical wires.

So I told him he's grounded.

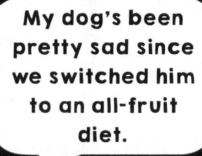

My dog's been pretty sad since we switched him to an all-fruit diet.

In fact, he's a little melon collie.

Have you heard the joke about peanut butter?

Nevermind, it's nuts and you'll spread it.

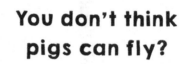

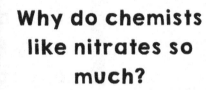

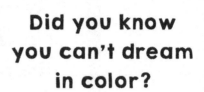

What kind of establishment handcuffs you while you eat?

Arresteraunt.

Women are not foolishg enough to eat Tide pods,

but it's hard to deter gents.

There's something wrong with this chair!

Maybe you're just having a bad chair day.

I almost fell down the stairs with a basket of laundry.

It was a clothes one.

Where do belly buttons go to college?

The Navel Academy.

Some people have commented that I smell like coins.

It's just my natural cents.

My daughter loves the work of Edgar Allan Poe.

She just can't stop raven about it.

In high school,
I tried to put my
grades up for
adoption.

Because I
couldn't raise
them on my own.

Why was the printer playing music?

The paper was jamming. Why did the printer stop making music? It ran out of toner.

A slice of apple pie costs $2.00 in Cuba and $3.00 in Puerto Rico.

These are the pie rates of the Caribbean.

What did the Italian math teacher say when his house was robbed?

"What the hexagon?"

Why should you never throw away an old dolphin?

Because they can easily be re-porpoised!

I'd like to tell dad jokes, but I don't have kids.

I guess that's a faux pa.

Made in the USA
Monee, IL
02 November 2019